SCIENCE IN OUR WORLD

SOUNDS
and
MUSIC

Contributory Author
Brian Knapp, BSc, PhD
Art Director
Duncan McCrae
Special photography
Graham Servante
Special models
Tim Fulford, Head of CDT, Leighton Park School
Editorial consultants
Anna Grayson, Rita Owen
Science advisor
*Jack Brettle, BSc, PhD, Chief Research Scientist,
Pilkington plc*
Environmental Education Advisor
Colin Harris, County Advisor, Herts. CC
Illustrators
Craig Walker, Angus McCrae and Mark Franklin
Production controller
Gillian Gatehouse
Print consultants
Landmark Production Consultants Ltd
Printed and bound in Hong Kong

Designed and produced by EARTHSCAPE EDITIONS,

First published in the United Kingdom in 1991
by Atlantic Europe Publishing Company Ltd,
86 Peppard Road, Sonning Common, Reading,
Berkshire, RG4 9RP, UK

Copyright © 1991
Atlantic Europe Publishing Company Ltd

British Library Cataloguing in Publication Data

Knapp, Brian
Sounds and music
1. Sounds and music – For children
I. Title   II. Series
534
ISBN 1-869860-25-X

In this book you will find some words that have been shown in **bold** type. There is a full explanation of each of these words on pages 46 and 47.

On many pages you will find experiments that you might like to try for yourself. They have been put in a coloured box like this.

Acknowledgements
The publishers would like to thank the following:
Micklands Primary School, Leighton Park School,
Hickies Limited, Chris Bayliss of VM records
Fafu Kingdon, Chan Chan, Alaistair McCrae
and Reading Music.

Picture credits
t=top b= bottom l=left r=right

All photographs from the Earthscape
Editions photographic library except
the following: Alan Cash Limited
18/19; Casio Electronics Limited
42; Chris Bayliss 43b; Erik
Pelham 44/45; Hutchison
Library 27; Oxford Scientific
Films Limited 11b;
Premaphotos Wildlife 8;
ZEFA 10, 17t, 17m,
17b, 22, 31, 35

Contents

Introduction

Listen carefully. Listen to the sounds of other people near to you. Listen more carefully and you will be able to hear sounds from further away. Perhaps you can hear the sound of traffic, or the countryside, or the sea. Now listen very carefully to yourself. You make sounds all the time. Listen for your breathing; for the sound as you move in your chair or as you turn the page.

Sounds are all around you. Sometimes you call them speech, sometimes music. If they are irritating sounds you call them **noise**. Some sounds you can ignore. Others make you listen.

scales
page 24

noise
page 22

reeds
page 34

decibels
page 16

guitar
page 42

In this book you will find out how sounds are made and how we hear them. You will understand why some sounds are pleasant and others harmful. You will discover how important sounds are to animals as well as to people.

There are some very unusual musical instruments shown in these pages. You may be able to see some more in your local museum. Many people also make their own instruments. These pages show you how you can make some for yourself.

Find out about the fascinating world of sound in any way you choose. Just turn to a page and begin your discoveries.

pipes
page 32

sound boxes
page 12

stereo
page 20

signals
page 8

brass
page 36

warnings
page 10

What is sound?

The world is made of many kinds of sounds. But high sounds and low sounds, sharp sounds and flat sounds, nice sounds and horrible sounds are all produced by **vibrations**.

Bony sound

A sound is a vibration that can be heard. It does not have to be in the air. Sometimes we can hear vibrations that travel through the bones of our body. Put a finger gently into each ear to block out the normal sounds. Now hum the deepest note you can manage. Make it a long single **note** using a big breath. Feel the sound get to your ears through your head.

Keep humming but now take your fingers out of your ears and see what happens.

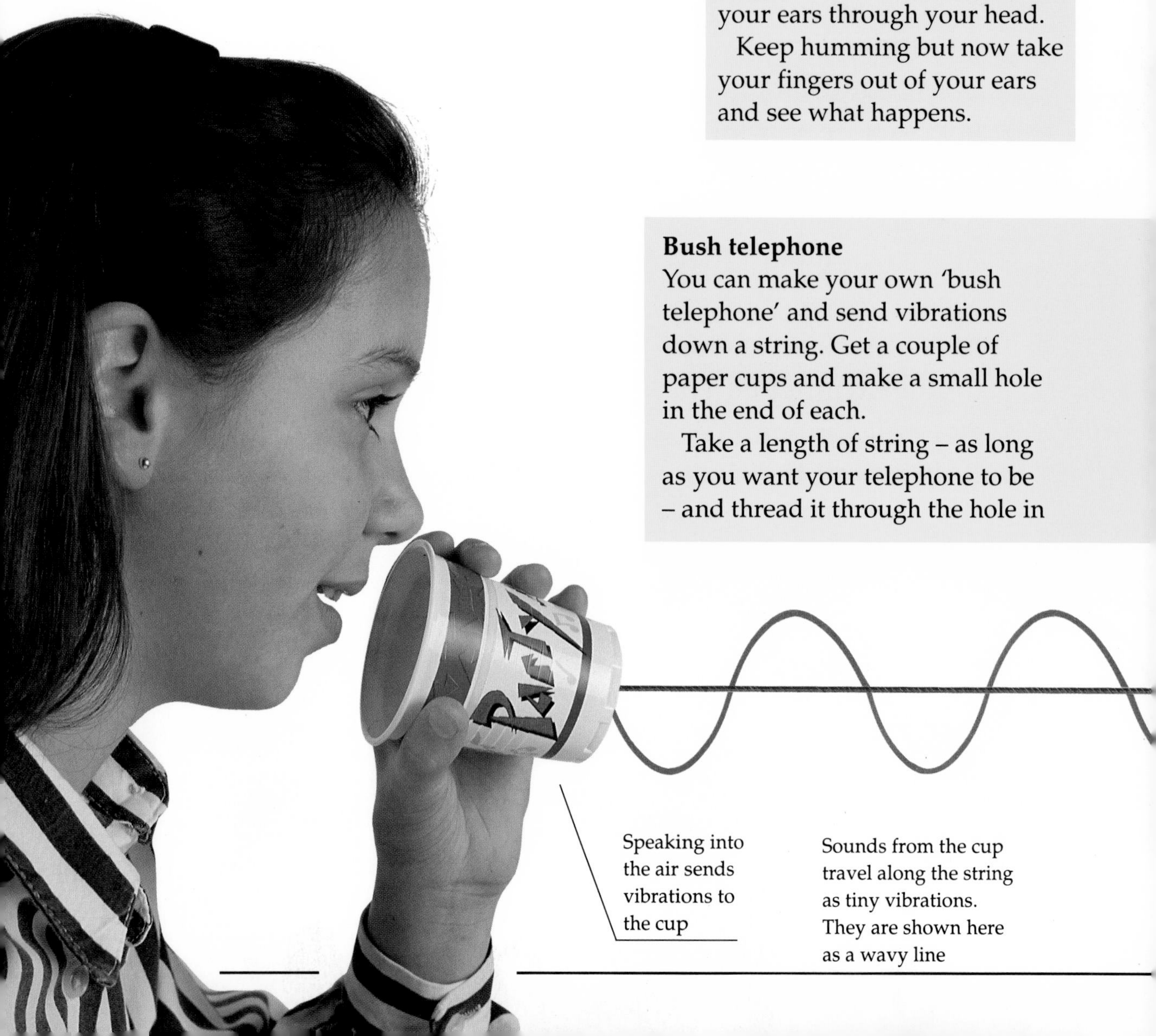

Bush telephone

You can make your own 'bush telephone' and send vibrations down a string. Get a couple of paper cups and make a small hole in the end of each.

Take a length of string – as long as you want your telephone to be – and thread it through the hole in

Speaking into the air sends vibrations to the cup

Sounds from the cup travel along the string as tiny vibrations. They are shown here as a wavy line

Make a noise

You can see how sounds are made in many ways. One of them is by blowing up a balloon. As you blow there is very little sound because the air enters slowly. But when you burst the balloon you hear a 'bang' sound because the air escapes very quickly.

Another common way to make a sound is to scrape a chair on a wooden floor. As the chair leg judders it moves the surrounding air, setting up vibrations. When the vibrations reach our ears we hear it as a rasping sound.

each cup. Then tie the ends off with a big knot.

Put your mouth to one cup and ask a friend to put the other cup over their ear. Walk apart until the string is stretched tight. If you speak into the cup your friend will be able to hear you.

Sounds that signal

Croaking for company
How does a male find a female in a forest? This frog from Australia has the answer.

It takes in a deep breath, swells out a pouch in its throat until it is almost doubled in size, and then uses it as a sounding board to make a deep croaking sound that can be heard for a long way.

Each frog has a different size of pouch and this means that its sounding board gives a special note. In a similar way people have different shaped mouths which help give each voice its own sound.

A sound always has a meaning. For example when the telephone rings it tells you there will be someone wanting to talk to you.

Sounds are just as important to animals, especially when they want to go courting or to set out their territory.

Bleating for comfort

Sheep bleat gently to tell their lambs where they are and that all is well.

If a fox or some other sign of danger appears in the distance the bleat changes note and says: 'Take care.'

Making sound signals

When we want to signal to people we use special words as well as changing the tone and loudness of our voices. But we can make many sound signals to each other without speaking a word.

Try making sounds that signal without speaking. Try a deep shout, then a high shout, then a short shout and finally a long one. Discover which causes the most attention, then try to work out why.

Do the same by clapping and then using a whistle. Can you think why sounds made by shouting, clapping and whistling mean something quite different?

The crow with two meanings

As soon as it is light the cock begins to crow. But the 'cock-a-doodle-doo' is not a chicken's form of yawn as it wakes up.

The cock is making important signals to other chickens. The cry says to female chickens: 'Come here, there is a friendly welcome.' At the same time it gives this signal to other males: 'Watch it lads – this is my patch.'

Warning sounds

Some sounds are very special because they give a warning. Many short sharp sounds are often warnings.

The wail of a siren, for example, sounds a warning: 'Give a clear route for the emergency vehicle.' A car horn is blown when the driver wants to warn other road users of danger. There are many others that you can probably think of.

Penetrating sounds
A warning sound has to be heard above the everyday sounds. It must tell people that something important is happening. This means the sound has to be very loud, but it also has to carry well.

Like the police car in the picture below, danger sounds are always shrill and harsh because a high note will carry well in air. It will even get through a closed window.

A common warning

We hear different kinds of warning sound in many places in our lives. Perhaps it is a bell or siren to tell us there is a fire alarm, or a whistle to remind us that the kettle is boiling. These sounds all have one thing in common – the sounds are shrill and piercing.

A hiss of danger

Snakes are timid creatures unless they are threatened. If a snake feels it is in danger it will rear up and face its attacker.

Some snakes – like the rattlesnake – have a special tail that makes a sound when it is shaken quickly. But the best sign most snakes can give is to hiss loudly. These signs of danger will make all but the most brave animals turn and flee.

Fooling the brain

The brain is best at picking up changes in sound. Unchanging notes will soon be ignored. Think how easy it is to ignore the sound of traffic as you walk down a busy street.

Warning sounds must change constantly so that the brain keeps alert to them. Many electronic clocks have alarms that send out several short high notes, then they pause, then send the notes again. This is designed to warn the brain to wake up.

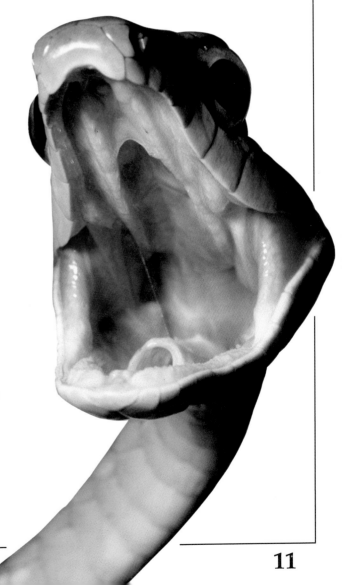

Strong vibrations

How much sound you hear depends on how much air you can vibrate. When you knock on a small piece of wood you get a small flat sound. But knock on a table top or a hollow door and the sound is much louder. This is because you have set a much larger piece of wood vibrating. You have made something that makes sounds louder, called an **amplifier**.

Boxes of sound
Many instruments would make tiny noises if they were not fitted with some kind of amplifier. Usually it is in the form of a **sound box**.

Sound boxes may be not always be easy to recognise. The sound box of a guitar, for example, is also used as the frame. The vibration goes from the strings through the bridge and into the hollow box below. This makes the whole box vibrate.

A 'tweeter' is the smallest speaker. Its job is to give out the very highest notes

A mid-range speaker is larger than a tweeter and it gives out the medium notes

The biggest speaker is called a 'woofer', and it gives out the deepest notes

Loudspeakers

A loudspeaker is a thin cone that vibrates when electrical signals are sent from a radio, television or tape player.

The cone of a loudspeaker sets up vibrations in the air and also in the loudspeaker case. The case acts as a sound box.

No single loudspeaker can produce all sounds well. This case has three speakers inside. Each one covers part of the sound range.

Feel the vibrations

Hold your hand against a loudspeaker case when it is working and you can feel the vibrations from the cone. If you press hard on the case you prevent the case from vibrating well and the sounds are less clear.

Large speakers are often placed on stands rather than directly on the soft carpeted floor of a room. Can you explain why?

Thumb piano

This small instrument from Africa is made using half a dried fruit – called a gourd – as a sound box. The pieces of old saw blade are stapled to the sound box and propped up on a nail.

Although it is very simple it can produce a pleasant sound. It is played by plucking the blades.

Sounds in your ear

Outer ear

The ear is a wonderful sound receiver. The part of the ear we can see has strange folds. These are designed to make the skin keep its funnel shape and let it capture even the tiniest vibrations.

Just inside our heads is a special system that lets the brain make sense of the trapped vibrations.

What can you hear?

The range of sounds we can hear is decided by the inner ear. People can hear sounds that range from a deep hum to a high screech.

Other creatures have differently shaped inner ears and they can hear a different range of sounds. Dogs, for example, can hear sounds that are outside our range.

Parts of the ear

Sound waves are funnelled down the trumpet-shaped outer ear to a sheet of skin called the **eardrum**. This works like a door, keeping the dirty outside world away from the sensitive inner ear.

The middle ear has three tiny bones that connect the ear drum to the inner ear.

The inner ear is a coiled tube filled with liquid and lined with tiny hairs of varying lengths. Each sound wave makes some of the hairs vibrate. The brain can tell what kind of sound has been heard from the way the hairs vibrate.

Bones of the middle ear

Coiled tube with sensor hairs of the inner ear

Eardrum

Cup your hands

When you want to hear something better you cup your hands over your ears. Without thinking about it you make your hands into a kind of funnel.

Try making a funnel out of a piece of paper wrapped into a cone. Does a bigger funnel work better than a small one? Does a funnel stop you hearing sounds from any direction?

Is it loud or soft?

It is impossible to get away from sound. Even in the quietest room there is sound filtering in from the outside. Our ears are so sensitive we can hear tiny sounds, such as when a pin drops onto a floor. But does this mean that our ears are too delicate to put up with very loud noises? Many people want to know 'how loud is *too* loud?'.

Why sounds are loud
The more effort, or **energy**, you put into making a sound, the louder it is. When you whisper, very little energy is used. When you talk normally more energy is needed. But when you shout or scream you open your mouth very wide to let as much energy as possible reach the air.

Beating **drums**, blowing a **trumpet** and shouting are all examples of sounds that get louder the more effort we put into them.

But machines use so much energy they can make far louder sounds. The scream of a jet engine can be heard over long distances because it uses enormous amounts of energy.

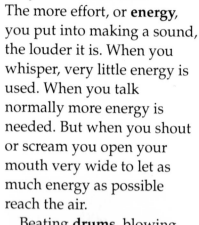

A sound scale

People can measure the amount of sound on a scale using a sound meter. Zero on the sound scale is when it seems perfectly quiet.

The sound scale is marked off in special units called **decibels**. A sound over 100 on the scale is almost painful. Here are some examples of the loudness of sounds that are common in our lives.

Damaging sound

Very loud sounds can damage or kill the tiny hairs of the inner ear. A large jet aircraft taking off can make a noise of nearly 140 decibels, well over the danger limit of 120.

Any loud sound can cause damage, even if it is enjoyable. That is why people who play their personal stereos loudly may find they have hearing problems after just a few months.

120 decibels

70 decibels

30 decibels

The scale of a sound meter

Room for echoes

When you make a sound in a room it is bounced, or reflected, off all the walls and the ceiling. Because sound travels slowly the bounced sound arrives some time after the original sound. This is called an **echo**.

Strong echoes can be a nuisance, but no echo at all makes the sound seem uninteresting. Buildings have to be designed to give just the right amount of echo.

Sydney Opera House

The Sydney Opera House in Australia is one of the world's largest opera houses. The time that the sound takes to bounce back from the walls could give strange echoes. To overcome this problem the building had to be designed to get the correct balance of echoes inside each of the five large halls.

Sound clouds

In many old halls echoes are a big problem. To improve matters huge plastic discs are hung from the ceiling. They are made to **absorb** sound and cut down the echoes.

Making echoes

Some places produce better echoes than others. A large cave with its hard curved walls makes an excellent place for echoes. Ask your teacher if you can try to make echoes in your school hall. Shout loudly at one wall and listen for the echoes.

If you do not get a good echo this might be because the hall is built in a special way. Look to see if there are any absorbing materials like curtains that might deaden the sounds.

Whispering spaces

Some buildings show the effect of echoes very well. Sounds travel better round a dome or in a tunnel than any other shape. This is the reason why, if you go to a large church, mosque or temple, even a whisper or the sound of footsteps may be heard tens of metres away.

Finding your way with sound

Our ears are like microphones. They pick up whatever sounds are around. Some are direct sounds, while other sounds reach the ear by being bounced off walls, floors and other objects. We need all the sounds to tell what our surroundings are like.

Brain waves

We have two ears to help our brains make sense of the sounds we hear.

As the brain hears a sound it decides which ear has picked up the loudest signal. This difference in loudness then lets the brain work out where the sound came from – left, behind, right or ahead of you.

Find the sound!

Have you ever heard a small insect like a mosquito buzzing around at night? Have you been irritated but can't find where the insect is?

Insects like this are very difficult to pinpoint because their buzzing can be heard when they are very close. This means you can only use one ear to find the insect. A single ear is not a good direction finder. So swat as you may, the chances are the insect will get away unharmed.

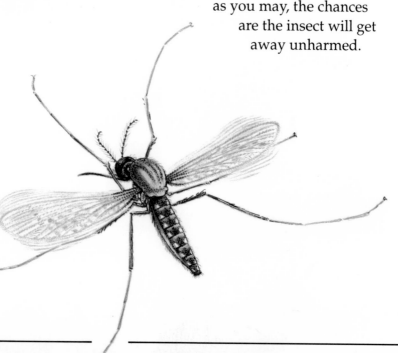

Where am I?

To find out how important these sounds are, clap your hands firmly over your ears so you keep all sounds out. Now stand up and shut your eyes. Try walking about, and you will soon discover that it is almost impossible. Take your hands away but keep your eyes closed. You can hear your feet move on the floor and many other sounds that tell you where things are.

The secret of stereo

Stereo is a common word used today. It means **stereophonic**, or 'all round', sound. To us this is 'normal' sound, because we hear all round all the time.

If you cover one ear you will soon discover that the world of 'one direction sound' is a much less interesting place.

Stereophonic sounds are produced by the headphones of your cassette player. In the studio where the sounds were recorded there were two microphones placed to pick up sounds just like your ears. The result is to put sound back into your ears in exactly the same way as it reached the microphones. This allows youto tell where each instrument was placed in the recording studio.

Keeping noise at bay

In today's busy world there are lots of sounds that annoy us. Some of these sounds – such as the sounds of traffic or an aeroplane taking off – can be so loud that they stop us concentrating. All unwanted sounds like these are called noise.

We cannot keep noise out of our live completely, but we can do some things to keep it at bay.

Brain filters noise
Our brains can filter out noise – unless it is exceptionally loud. This is because the brain is only interested in change. This is the reason people can work in a noisy placeor why we can hear a sound we are interested in – perhaps someone talking – even in a noisy street.

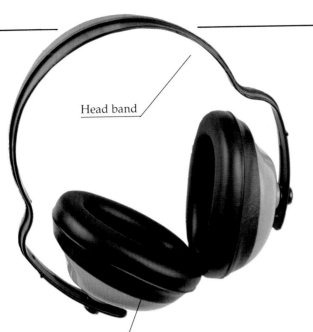

Head band

Padded earpiece

No room for noise
Is the room where you are sitting noisy? If so it means the walls and ceiling are bouncing all the sounds about. Quiet rooms have materials in them which soak up – or absorb – the sound. Curtains and wallpaper are very good at soaking up sounds. So are the books in a library. Try shouting at different types of surface to find the best ones that absorb the sound.

Noise muffs
Many people have to work close to noisy machines. If they did not protect themselves in some way the noise would eventually make them deaf.

In many noisy places people now have to wear special protective **ear muffs**. These look like headphones but their job is to keep noise out. Inside the ear muffs there are special materials that absorb much of the noise. They do not keep all the noise out, however, because people need a little sound to help them keep their balance or work machines safely.

Let's make music

Music is part of our way of life. It has been made in all parts of the world for thousands of years.

But although we all like music, and we can all sing songs, most of us cannot make up, or compose tunes. So what is it that makes music? On this page you will find some of the most important patterns that build together into the music we enjoy.

Music shorthand
All the notes used in music can be set out in a clever shorthand form as shown by the symbols on this page. It contains all the information that a musician needs, yet it is so simple it can be read at great speed.

doh
C

ray
D

me
E

Low pitch

Keeping in scale
The sounds that musical instruments make all form part of a pattern called a **musical scale**.

Sing out the musical scale 'doh ray me fah so la te doh' above, as you would in a music lesson. Now you have sung an **octave**, that is a range of eight notes each higher than the last. The notes at the top and bottom of the scale are both doh. You sang the last doh with twice as high a note as the first.

All these notes are pleasing on the ear. We use them – and their higher and lower cousins – to make music.

Take a note

There are many types of sound. Musicians call a single sound that does not vary a note. Musicians use the word **pitch** to describe how high or low a note is. A high note, the sort of thing you might make by twanging a short string has a *high* pitch, a deep note, formed by plucking a long string, has a *low* pitch.

Keeping time

Clap your hands in a regular way. It makes a simple, but quite interesting **beat**. Now clap your hands in an irregular manner. Its not such an interesting sound is it? It is the regular nature of sounds, the **rhythm**, that carries us forward with the music.

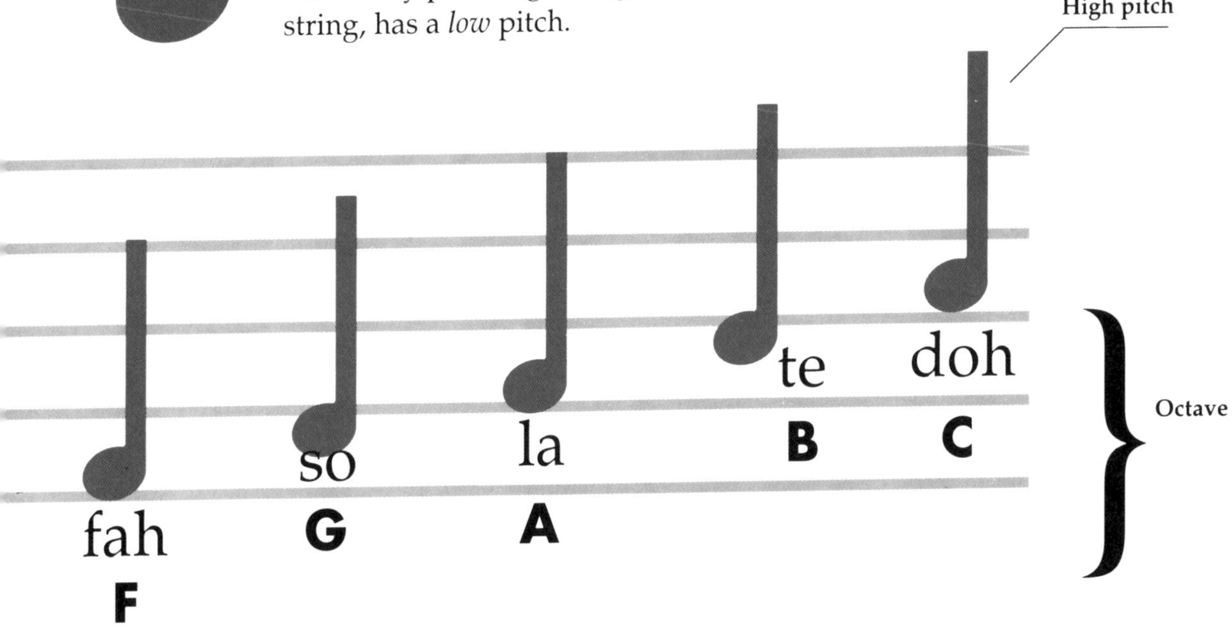

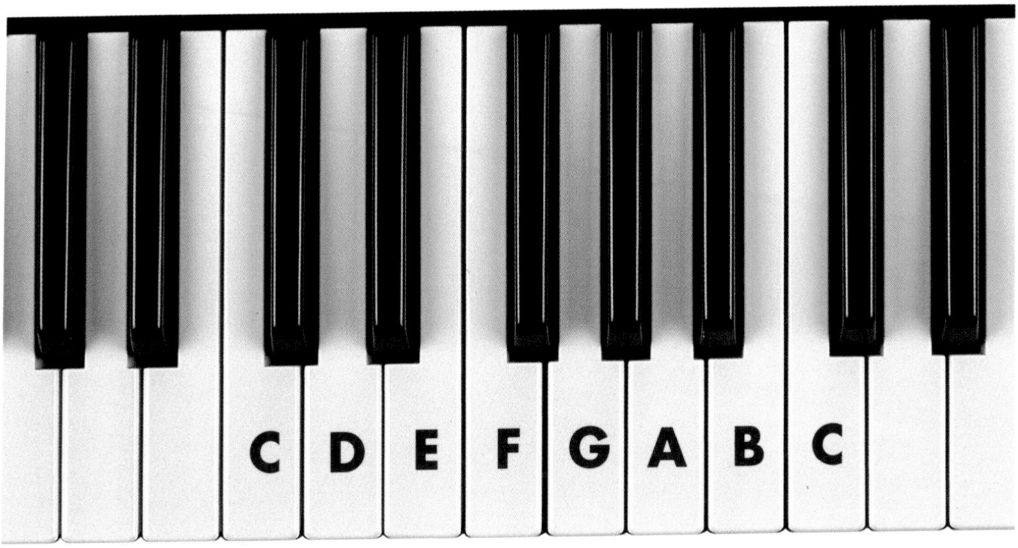

High pitch

doh

te

C

B

la

A

so

G

fah

F

Octave

C D E F G A B C

Musical sticks

The simplest musical instrument is easy to find. It can be your desk, the floor or the walls. You make it work by tapping or thumping using your hands. Now you have a simple vibrating board – a kind of hitting, or **percussion**, instrument. Some others are shown below.

The xylophone
The **xylophone** is a musical instrument made up of sticks of different lengths. They are placed on a frame and hit with special hammers. The sound they make is amplified and made more rich by the tubes or globes hanging below.

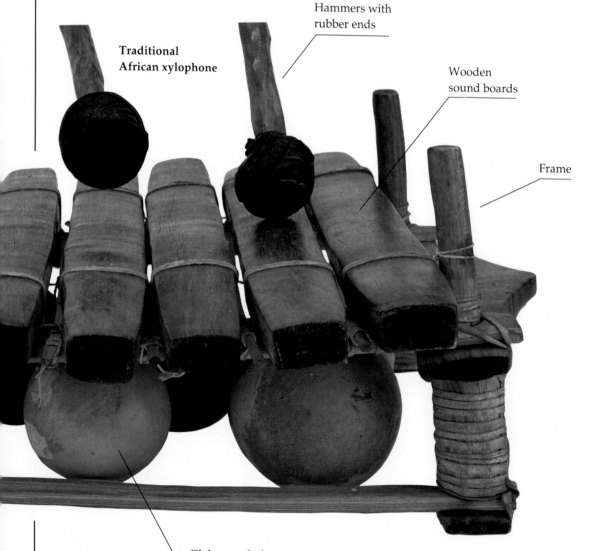

Traditional
African xylophone

Hammers with
rubber ends

Wooden
sound boards

Frame

Globes made from
seed cases (gourds)

Dropping sticks

If you drop a small piece of wood on a hard floor it will make a sound. Ask a grown-up to cut pieces of wood of different lengths. Drop them on the floor to hear the note they make. Can you make a scale by dropping the pieces in order, starting with the longest and finishing with the shortest?

Striking bottles

Get eight clean empty bottles and put them in a row. Pour different amounts of water into each of them. Tap the side of each bottle with a pencil to make a note.

Ask a grown-up to help you to 'tune' your bottle xylophone by adding or removing water until you have a musical scale. Can you then play the tune 'Ten Green Bottles' by tapping gently on the bottles in the right order?

Gamelan

Percussion bands are found in all countries of the world. One of the best known is the **gamelan** orchestra from Java in South East Asia. Here a group of men play a wide range of xylophones and other instruments.

Bang out the sounds

Instruments that we beat have a special place in our lives. Beating, or percussion, instruments are easy to use to keep a rhythm while walking, marching, or even dancing. This is why they have been used throughout the world, in ancient times as well as modern.

Maracas
Maracas are rattles made by putting some beads or hard seeds inside hollowed out wood.

Maracas are played with one in each hand, shaking them to help make the musical rhythm. The larger the maracas, the deeper the note made.

Hand-held drum
A drum is a sound box with a skin stretched across one end. It produces only one note. The bigger the skin, the slower the skin vibrates and the deeper the note made.

This hand-held drum has little discs on the side. It is called a tambourine. It is played with the tips of the fingers and the heels of the hands.

Crash the cymbals
Cymbals for use in orchestras come in twos. They are discs of metal that are clapped together to make a loud crashing sound. It is the musical version of thunder.

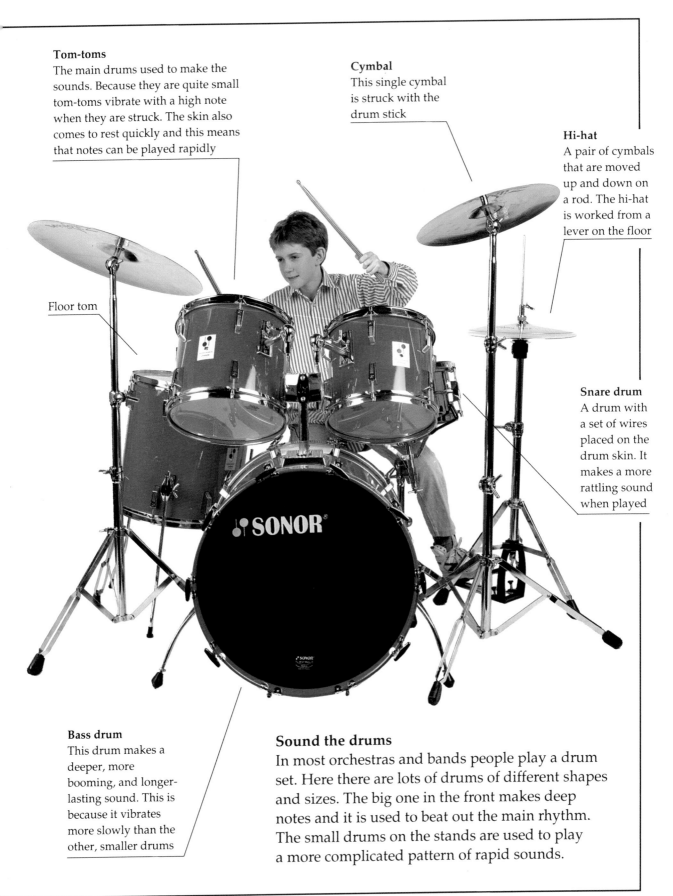

Tom-toms
The main drums used to make the sounds. Because they are quite small tom-toms vibrate with a high note when they are struck. The skin also comes to rest quickly and this means that notes can be played rapidly

Cymbal
This single cymbal is struck with the drum stick

Hi-hat
A pair of cymbals that are moved up and down on a rod. The hi-hat is worked from a lever on the floor

Floor tom

Snare drum
A drum with a set of wires placed on the drum skin. It makes a more rattling sound when played

Bass drum
This drum makes a deeper, more booming, and longer-lasting sound. This is because it vibrates more slowly than the other, smaller drums

Sound the drums
In most orchestras and bands people play a drum set. Here there are lots of drums of different shapes and sizes. The big one in the front makes deep notes and it is used to beat out the main rhythm. The small drums on the stands are used to play a more complicated pattern of rapid sounds.

Strike a chord

When several sounds are played together they often make a **chord**. Most stringed instruments are very good at playing chords because they are often made up of several 'instruments'.

String makes the sound when hit by the hammer

Hammer strikes the string and causes it to vibrate

Damper stops the string vibrating

Jack rises and flicks the hammer at the string

Piano
A piano has many strings all held in a frame. When you press a key on the keyboard, levers make a hammer hit a string quickly.

The piano is actually 88 separate instruments all put together in one frame. You need a separate hammer – and therefore a separate key – for each note.

Key is pressed by the finger

Lutes and guitars

There are many hand-held instruments that are played by plucking the strings. The lute shown below was made in Africa and it has part of a lizard skin for its sound box. The back of the sound box was carved out of a piece of tree trunk and the stem was made from bamboo. Plucking the strings with the fingers gives a chord.

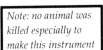

Note: no animal was killed especially to make this instrument

Pulling strings

A **harp** is like a piano without the keyboard. The strings are plucked directly to make a sound.

The sound box of the harp is the long sloping base. The pillar is used to support the frame because the strings have to be pulled very tight.

At first sight the **harpsichord** looks like a piano because its frame is laid flat and it has a keyboard. However, the strings are plucked by special levers that are connected to the keys. It is therefore most closely related to the harp. The keyboard, however, makes it easier to play notes quickly.

Blow for all you are worth!

If you take a tube and blow into it nothing happens. This may seem strange, because all wind instruments – such as trumpets, recorders and even organs – work this way. One trick is to blow over the edge of the tube not down it. This sets up vibrations of the air in the tube which we hear as a note.

Mouthpiece

Slot shaped to make the air hit the edge of the tube and vibrate

Make a musical pipe
Take a clean bottle and hold the open end to your mouth. Blow across it and you will hear a deep sound. You have made a simple musical pipe!

Find some more bottles the same size as the first and fill them to different levels with water. When you blow across each one in turn, you will produce a number of different notes.

Open holes are closed directly by the fingers to change the length of the vibrating pipe

Mouth hole

Recorder

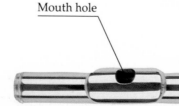

The recorder

Blowing over the edge of the tube can be made easier by a special mouthpiece.

A recorder has a mouthpiece that makes sure the air you blow hits the edge of the tube and sets up vibrations that make the sound.

The flute

A **flute** is one of the wind 'pipe' instruments. There is a mouth hole in the side and you blow across it. The different notes are made by covering and uncovering the holes in the side. This is much easier than using a set of pipes and it gives a richer sound.

Pan-pipes

The South American **Pan-pipes** are simple pipes and the sound is made by blowing across the top of each one. Because you blow over the pipes they have a haunting 'breathy' sound.

Pipe lengths

Every one of the pipes is cut to a different length. Each pipe vibrates in just the right way to make all the notes on the scale. The longest lengths give the slowest vibration and the deepest note.

This key is worked with the little finger using a lever

These keys are worked directly by the fingers

This bar holds all the keys over the holes in the flute

Flute

Pan-pipes

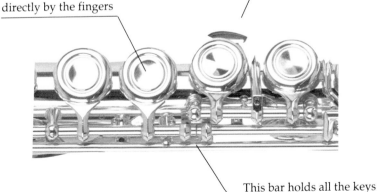

Bags of reeds

A **reed** is a small device for making vibrations. It gives a squawking sound.

Some people can make a reed from a flat blade of grass by pulling it gently apart to make a slit in the centre. When they hold it to their lips and blow they make the edges of the grass vibrate.

Reeds can be used to make fine sounds as well, and they are used in many musical instruments.

Reeds
This selection of reeds come from an oboe (top), a **bagpipe**, a clarinet and a **saxophone** (bottom)

Make a reedy sound
It is easy to make a reed from a drinking straw. Flatten about two centimetres of one end.

Cut a tiny piece off each corner, pop the flattened piece inside your mouth, moisten it a little and blow hard. You should be able to make a harsh squawking sound.

Party blower. Does the note change as the blower gets longer?

Bagpipes

As the piper blows air into a bag – made from a sheep's stomach – the reed pipe is fed with air from the bag. The other pipes are called drones. They work all the time to give a background sound.

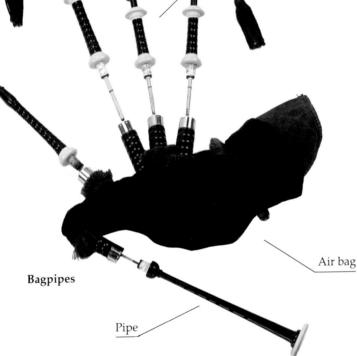

Drones

Air bag

Bagpipes

Pipe

Saxophone

The saxophone

The saxophone – or 'sax' for short – is used to make a very mellow loud sound. It was invented over a century ago as an instrument for a military band.

On the sax in this picture you can see how the length of the vibrating pipe is changed by pressing down or releasing pads that cover the holes. The pads are worked using keys.

Blow your own trumpet

A trumpet is a member of the **brass** family of instruments. When you look into the mouth piece there is simply a hole. If you blow into the hole nothing happens. All the sounds that come from these instruments are made by making your lips into a vibrating reed.

Lugbara horn
In this unusual **horn** the lips are put inside the hole before blowing. It gives a deep resounding sound.

Conch shell
This is the simplest of all trumpets. To make one you need a conch shell from the seaside. You make a small hole near the closed end and blow. It needs a lot of skill but if you can make it work the sound is really haunting.

Lips are placed in the mouthpiece here

Bugles, horns and trumpets
The simplest brass instruments are **bugles** and hunting horns. The trumpet (shown below) is a horn that has been modified with valves to make a wider range of notes.

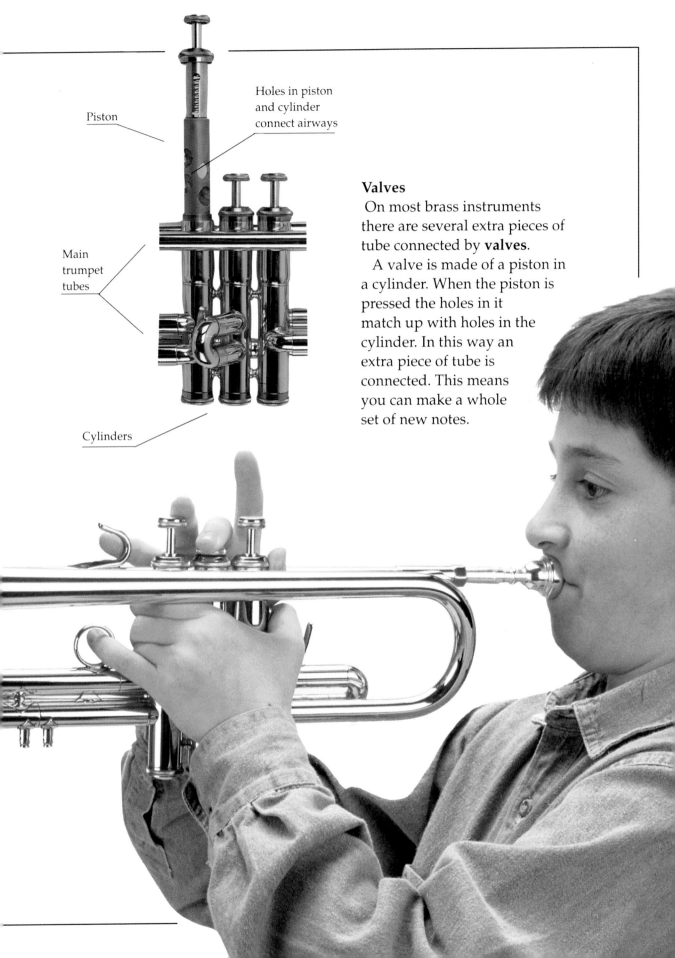

Piston

Holes in piston
and cylinder
connect airways

Main
trumpet
tubes

Cylinders

Valves

On most brass instruments there are several extra pieces of tube connected by **valves**.

A valve is made of a piston in a cylinder. When the piston is pressed the holes in it match up with holes in the cylinder. In this way an extra piece of tube is connected. This means you can make a whole set of new notes.

Singing strings

One way to make a stretched string vibrate is to draw a **bow** across it. This action seems to make the string sing in a special way. There are many instruments that can do this.

Bow made of horse hair

Hole in violin case

Fingerboards
The bow makes the string vibrate, but to get a range of notes you need many lengths of string. By pressing your fingers down in special places on the fingerboard you can alter the length of vibrating string to get every note in the scale.

Fingerboard

Pegs for tightening the strings

Let the sound come through
The hole in the **violin** is extremely important and has to be in just the right place and of just the right size. It lets the sounds out of the box.

Try covering up the hole of a string instrument and it will seem quite flat and uninteresting. It will also be much quieter.

Rosin

This strange substance is called **rosin**. It is rubbed on the bow before playing. It gives just the right amount of slip so that the bow makes the strings vibrate very quickly.

Double bass

Point

Secrets of the bow

To play one of the violin family you normally use a bow.

The bow consists of a wooden stick shaped into a curve. The string is made of many horse hairs tied between two posts. The one at the top is called the point and the lower one is called the frog. The frog can be moved slightly in order to tension the bow.

A family of strings

People sometimes call stringed instruments 'fiddles'. There is a wide range of stringed instruments and they make a family. The largest is the double bass. Slightly smaller is the 'cello. Both these instruments are played held upright.

The viola comes next, then the violin. These instruments are small enough to be tucked under the chin.

Frog

Sing up

Nature has given us a marvellous musical instrument to play. It has many of the same pieces as a man-made musical instrument but it can do far more. We use it all the time – its called our voice.

Take a deep breath

How long can you talk without taking a breath? You will soon find that talking uses lots of air. To make sounds we have to move air through our throats. Our 'music' can be speech or singing, but it always starts when air from our lungs moves quickly to our mouths.

Making the sound

Near the top of our throat are two small flaps of skin which act like a reed. They are called the **vocal chords**. When air goes past the vocal chords they vibrate.

The small squeaking sound goes into our mouths. The mouth is a sound box and it makes the sound bigger and richer.

A conductor of a choir often asks us to open our mouths wide. He wants our 'sound box' to give the biggest sound we can!

Head bent down to get a low note by changing the shape of the throat

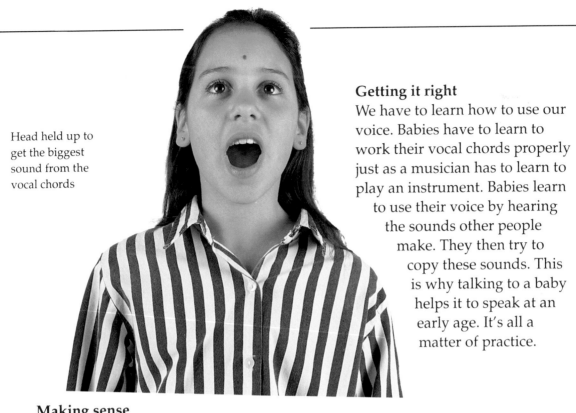

Head held up to get the biggest sound from the vocal chords

Getting it right

We have to learn how to use our voice. Babies have to learn to work their vocal chords properly just as a musician has to learn to play an instrument. Babies learn to use their voice by hearing the sounds other people make. They then try to copy these sounds. This is why talking to a baby helps it to speak at an early age. It's all a matter of practice.

Making sense

Speaking or singing is all about getting our message across in the shortest possible time.

Listen to a bird singing. It makes many short notes that give a pattern. This sound can be heard over a long distance and against a noisy background.

When we speak we do just the same. Each word is made up of many short sounds. Our brain changes these sound patterns into a message and matches it to patterns that have been memorised before.

Electrifying sound

For many centuries people made the best use of natural materials to make sound. But the electronic age has changed all this. Powerful electronic amplifiers can replace the sound box. The result has been to change what musical instruments look like and sound like.

Electric guitar

Fingerboard

Painted finish

Pick-ups

Foot controls

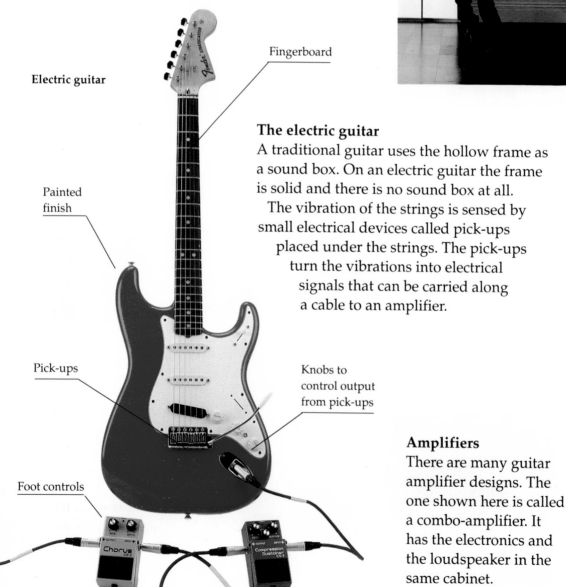

The electric guitar

A traditional guitar uses the hollow frame as a sound box. On an electric guitar the frame is solid and there is no sound box at all.

The vibration of the strings is sensed by small electrical devices called pick-ups placed under the strings. The pick-ups turn the vibrations into electrical signals that can be carried along a cable to an amplifier.

Knobs to control output from pick-ups

Amplifiers

There are many guitar amplifier designs. The one shown here is called a combo-amplifier. It has the electronics and the loudspeaker in the same cabinet.

Slider controls

Rhythm generator

Synthesizer

Synthesizers

Modern electronic sound often comes from keyboard-like instruments. They are really special computers. A rhythm generator, for example, makes up a continuous background rhythm. Some computers – called synthesizers – can make up totally new sounds. Others can listen to, or 'sample', a real instrument and then store the sound in their memories. They can then make a whole range of notes just from the small sample.

Sampler

Amplifier
and controls

Speaker
cabinet

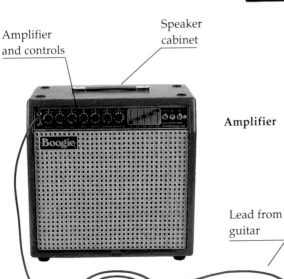

Amplifier

Lead from
guitar

The pop band

In a modern pop band the lead guitarist (right) and the keyboard player (background) will play the main notes of the tune. If there is a drummer and bass guitarist they can give extra rhythm to the music. But even this small band can make as many sounds as a whole orchestra by using their synthesizers.

Making a recording

This book tells you about many kinds of musical instrument. Recordings are made to that people can hear music whenever they want.

To record music properly needs a special recording studio filled with the latest kinds of computer.

Recording studios

Modern recording studios are quite compact and can easily fit inside an ordinary room. Everything is programmed in, synthesized and mixed inside computers. All the sounds are put onto wide tapes or computer disks. These master recordings then go to a factory and are used to make the records, compact discs (CDs) and cassettes you buy in the shops.

Slider controls are used by the recording operator to balance the loudness of each instrument or synthesizer, to fade sounds in and out and create many other special effects

Live and not so live

There is a special 'live' room where musicians sing or play their traditional instruments. It is sound-proofed to make sure the only sounds that reach the microphones come from the musicians.

Live rooms and control rooms do not even have to be in the same country. Live recordings and accompaniments do not have to happen at the same time. The trick is simply getting computers to talk to each other!

The sounds of the live voices and instruments are added to (or 'dubbed' over) the synthesized sound to make the final master recording on this 24-track tape recorder

Control room loudspeakers tell the operator what the final recording sounds like

A control room console

Outboard processing machines are computers that add a wide variety of sounds to the recording. You can ask for drums and many other sounds or you make echoes and lots of other special effects just by flicking a switch

New words

absorb
to soak up the sound.
Some of the best
absorbing materials are
those with rough surfaces
or those with holes

amplifier
something which makes
sounds louder

bagpipes
a musical reed instrument
that is pumped with air
supplied from an animal
bladder

beat
a sound made regularly.
The beat helps to
maintain the rhythm and
keeps the musical time

bow
an instrument used for
making strings vibrate.
Bows only work if they
are coated with rosin and
make rapid juddering
movements

brass
musical instruments
played by the mouth
using the lips as a reed

bugle
a kind of simple horn
designed for playing
military tunes

chord
the effect you get when
you play three or more
notes at the same time

decibel
a unit that gives a
measure of the loudness
of a sound

drum
A sound box with a
skin stretched across it.
It is hit with the hand
or sticks

eardrum
The flap of skin inside
the ear that acts as a
sounding board for
vibrations in the air

ear muffs
special 'headphones'
that have sound
deadening material
inside each ear cup

echoes
the indirect sound we
hear when vibrations are
bounced from an object

energy
the amount of effort needed
to get something done

flute
a woodwind instrument
without a mouthpiece.
Sound is made by blowing
across a mouth hole

gamelan
an Asian (Indonesian)
orchestra which consists
mainly of xylophone-type
instruments and bells

harp
a string instrument held
upright while the strings
are plucked

harpsichord
a piano-like keyboard
instrument where the
strings are plucked

horn
a tube-like instrument. It
was originally a hollowed
out animal horn

musical scale
a series of notes arranged in order

noise
any loud sound that is thought to be unpleasant

note
a single sound. Notes are often played together to make chords. Pleasing patterns of notes make music

octave
the gap between two notes, the upper one being twice as high as the lower

pan-pipes
South American bamboo pipes that are mounted in sets of differing lengths

percussion
the name for any instrument that makes a sound when it is struck

pitch
the name used to say how high or low the note is

reed
a small piece of material that vibrates when air is blown across it

rhythm
the way the music is set out in time

rosin
special sticky material made from turpentine

saxophone
a reed instrument with a curved and bell shaped end

sound box
a form of amplifier that is used to make musical instruments louder

stereophonic
a system for recording and playing sound using two or more microphones and loudspeakers

trumpet
a brass wind instrument. The sounds are made by shaping the lips in a special way against the trumpet mouthpiece

valve (musical)
a device which opens and closes over holes in wind instruments. There are many kinds of valve. Some are simple flaps over holes such as in the flute, whereas others are worked by pistons, such as in brass instruments

vibration
a regular pattern of movements. Sound waves are vibrations

violin
a string instrument played with a bow

vocal chords
the part of the lower throat that has two flaps of skin that vibrate as air flows over them. The vocal chords are used with the mouth to form many types of sound

xylophone
a percussion instrument made of a row of tuned wooden or metal blocks that are hit with sticks

Index